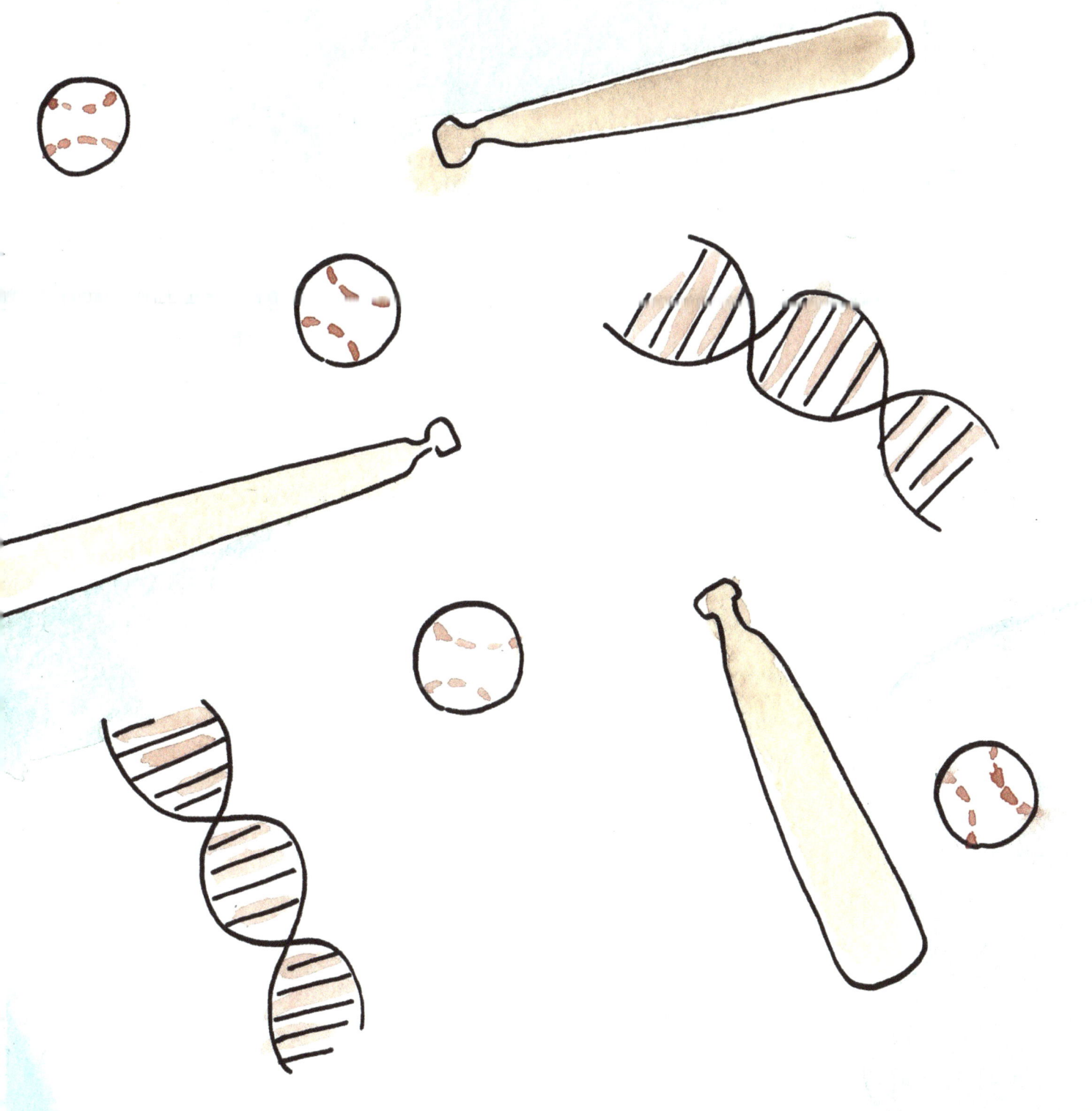

Copyright © 2021 Jeff Hansen

All rights reserved. No part of this book may be reproduced, distributed, or transmitted in any form or by any means, electronic or mechanical, including photocopying and recording, without the prior written permission from the publisher, except in the case of brief quotations embodied in critical reviews and certain other noncommercial uses permitted by copyright law.

The views and opinions expressed within this book are solely the author's own and do not necessarily express the views and opinions of Washington University in St. Louis nor Washington University in St. Louis School of Medicine.

This is a work of fiction. All of the names, characters, places, and events in this book are the work of our collective imagination. Any resemblance to actual persons, living or dead, or actual events is purely coincidental.

ISBN: 978-0-578-86340-5 (Hardcover)

Jeff Hansen is an MD-PhD student at Washington University in St. Louis. He thinks and writes about the human genome from the research laboratory, the hospital, and cozy coffee stops around St. Louis.

Find more of his writing at:
https://www.genomejeff.com/

Illustrations, cover image, and design completed by Aleyna Moeller.

Aleyna Moeller is an American illustrator based in Paris, France. She works traditionally with watercolor and ink, capturing sweet, playful stories and memories of travel.

Find more of her work at:
http://www.aleynamoeller.com/

All profits from this book will be donated to genetic and genomic charitable and research foundations.

THE PERFECT BASEBALL PLAYER

Written by Jeff Hansen - Illustrated by Aleyna Moeller

The sun rose from the sea ten minutes early, eager to begin her long list of chores. She first peeked through my window to wake me and greet me and remind me that it was time to prepare for my baseball game. She then moved on to the field to warm the grass and dry the infield dirt.

I sprung from bed, threw on my Rascals uniform, and began to chant: **"2! 4! 10 RUNS WE'LL SCORE!"** We were in the championship game against the Skippers. They live on the neighboring island and have won the tournament five years in a row. I painted thick black stripes underneath my eyes and finished the chant: **"6! 8! 'CAUSE TOGETHER WE'RE GREAT!"**

Flying down the stairs two at a time, I skidded to a stop at the entrance to the kitchen, surprised to find Grammie. "Fruit first Ana, questions after," she instructed before I could ask about Mom and Dad's absence. She watched me take a bite and then delivered the news, "You're officially a big sister!" I jumped from my chair and threw my arms to the sky in celebration. She continued, "Louis was born in the middle of the night. He and your parents are still at the hospital."

"What's he look like?" I asked. Grammie pulled out a picture that Mom and Dad had sent. He had happy blue eyes and a tuft of dark curly hair. "He's perfect..." I whispered. I wanted to know everything. "Will he be tall? Or fast? Will he play shortstop like me?" Grammie smiled and replied, "We can't predict those sorts of things, but doctors can predict if he'll grow sick, and then they can fix the problem! Have I ever told you about genes or genomes?" I thought for a moment but then shook my head back and forth.

HE IS A BOY

HE HAS B

Grammie walked over and taped the picture to the fridge. "Imagine the fridge is Lou." I giggled and asked, "So he's a cool kid, huh?" She ignored my joke and started arranging the colorful magnetic letters on the fridge into short sentences. "A gene is a sentence of special letters that describe some part of Lou." Grammie began, as she pointed to the magnetic letters.

"HE HAS BROWN HAIR"

"...UE EYES"

"Those are three genes: the boy gene, the blue-eyes gene, and the brown-hair gene." Then, she grabbed some yarn from the drawer. "And these special letters are made of DNA, which looks like yarn! It's a squiggly, microscopic mess." She used the magnets to hold up the yarn. "And all of the genes together," she pointed again to the three sentences, "is the genome!"

I think I understood. "It's like a story," I began, "but instead of paper, it's written on tiny pieces of DNA." I pointed at the yarn. "And just like sentences describe the main character in a story, each gene describes a part of me, or you, or Lou." I pointed at the three sentences that Grammie had written. "Finally, if you put all of the genes together, it's a genome. The story of us." Grammie nodded proudly, "Precisely, Ana."

"If the doctors can read the sentences, can they write new ones?" I asked. Grammie looked at me curiously, "What would you write?" I went over to the fridge and used some more letters to write: HE IS TALL. Grammie watched me spell the sentence and then responded, "Usually, we don't change anything unless the baby is going to be sick. Let me show you."

She opened the fridge door and closed it hard enough to cause some of the letters to fall off. "If doctors discover missing or incorrect letters that will cause the baby to be sick, they can put the words back together," she said as she picked up the letters from the ground and put them back onto the fridge.

 BLU EYE S

I marveled at how smart she was and asked, "How do you know all of this?" She explained, "Before you were born, it was my research team that discovered how to find and correct mistakes in the genome!" I should have guessed at that one.

10

Grammie glanced at the clock and said, "Lesson's over! It's time for your game!" I was so caught up in Grammie's science lesson that I had forgotten about baseball! I gave Grammie a big hug and grabbed my bag. "Your dad is waiting for you at the field. I'll meet you after the game at the hospital!" I hopped on my bike, gave her a salute, and sped away.

As I pedaled up to the field, I saw Dad sitting in the bleachers. "Hiya Ana!" He put out his hands for our pregame high-five handshake. Then, his face grew serious as he told me, "I hate to miss the game Ana, but I need to return to the hospital." My heart skipped a beat, and I asked, "Is something wrong?" Dad replied, "Louis is happy and healthy, but when the doctors read his genome this morning, they discovered a mistake that means he'll never be able to walk."

I burst out crying. I couldn't help it. Ever since Mom and Dad told me that I was going to have a baby brother, I dreamt of playing catch in the backyard or having batting practice in the field down the street. Now because of a small mistake in an important gene, none of that was possible. "Can't they fix it? Grammie said that doctors can put the letters back."

Dad kept his hands on my shoulders and told me, "Just because we can fix something doesn't mean we always should. Changing someone's genome is a big deal! Let's all talk to the doctors after the game. We won't make a decision without you." I nodded and wiped the tears from my face. He said, "In the meantime, I have a good feeling that this is the year that you'll beat the Skippers!"

14

The Skippers must have overheard Dad and set out to prove him wrong. In the first three innings, they scored 9 runs. 9-0. Is it possible that they grew even taller and stronger in the past year? I slumped down onto the dugout's bench and didn't notice when my best friend Esto plopped down next to me and began chattering away.

"Now everyone knows that the secret to a comeback is home runs. And everyone knows that the secret to home runs is big muscles. And the secret to big muscles?" He pulled out his bag of sunflower seeds, dumped the remaining contents into his mouth, and continued his pep talk, "Sunflower seeds!" When I didn't respond, he looked over, noticed the streaks in my eye paint, and slid closer to me on the bench, "What's wrong, Ana?"

I let out all of my feelings in a rush. "My brother was born this morning, and I want to be happy and play baseball and meet him and make this the best day ever, but the doctors said he won't be able to walk! So how can I play baseball and have fun knowing that he'll never be able to play himself!" Esto jumped off the bench, "Congrats Ana! Your brother will be okay! He's got the best sister in the whole wide world." I half smiled but remained on the bench.

Esto continued, "But you're wrong! He CAN still play baseball! Just imagine how good he'll be at throwing or hitting because he doesn't need to worry about running!" I wasn't convinced, "But how will he run to first base or chase down fly balls?" Esto gestured to the rest of the team around us, "That's why we have a team! Whatever he can't do, we'll do for him!"

Maybe Esto had a point. I was still a little sad, but as long as Lou has teammates, maybe it'll be okay. Lou can do what he's good at, and his teammates can do what they're good at. "Hey! That's how we can beat the Skippers! Esto you're a genius!" Esto shrugged, "Old news, Ana, old news."

I gathered the team around me. "The secret isn't more home runs! That's what the Skippers are best at, not us. If we all do what we're best at," I pointed to each of our different teammates, "running or fielding or hitting or pitching, then when you put us all together, we'll be unstoppable!" I put my hand in the middle and yelled, **"2! 4!"** And they yelled back, **"10 RUNS WE'LL SCORE!"** I continued, **"6! 8!"** And we all screamed, **"'CAUSE TOGETHER WE'RE GREAT!"**

With that, we roared back onto the field. And working as a team, we began to score runs. But with each run, the Skippers became more frustrated. Between innings, I noticed one especially upset player and walked over to him. "Exciting game!" I said. He sighed and responded, "Baseball's no fun when everyone just wants us to be tall and strong and hit homerun after homerun." I was puzzled and asked him, "You don't like hitting homeruns?"

It was the last inning, the game was tied 9-9, and I was on first base. Esto walked to the plate and hit the ball into the corner of the outfield. He wasn't fast, but he was strong. As soon as he hit it, I ran all the way from first base to score the game-winning run. I wasn't strong, but I was fast.

As I slid across home plate in a swirl of dust, my teammates swarmed out of the dugout to lift me onto their shoulders. We had won the game! And we had done it by using what was special about each of us.

After the game, I biked to the hospital. As I admired the grapefruit trees along the road, I remembered what Grammie had told me: "Cut a grapefruit tree skinny, and it will grow tall. Cut a grapefruit tree short, and it will grow wide. But no matter the size or shape, the grapefruit will always taste great." It's super cool that Grammie figured out how to change genes, but maybe we should only do it if someone's going to be really sick, or if the grapefruit isn't going to grow at all.

Lou may not be able to walk, but that means he can be better at something else. Like Esto said, Lou doesn't need to be the best at everything when he has teammates! Plus, why should I, or Mom, or Dad, be the one to decide what Lou is good or bad at? What if he doesn't even like what we end up picking! I thought the Skippers would have liked being tall and strong, but I was wrong.

When I arrived at the hospital covered in dirt and carrying the game ball that I was awarded, I found Dad in the lobby. "I knew it was your year!" he said as we performed another complicated handshake. "Dad, don't change anything about Lou." He smiled and put his arm around me as we walked down the hallway. "Your mom and I agree."

When I walked into the room, Lou looked over and his happy blue eyes seemed to grow even happier. I sat down next to him and handed him the game ball. "This one's for you Lou. If you want to be a pitcher, I'll be your catcher. If you want to be a catcher, I'll be your pitcher. 'Cause me, I'm your number one fan. And you, you're perfect."

THE END

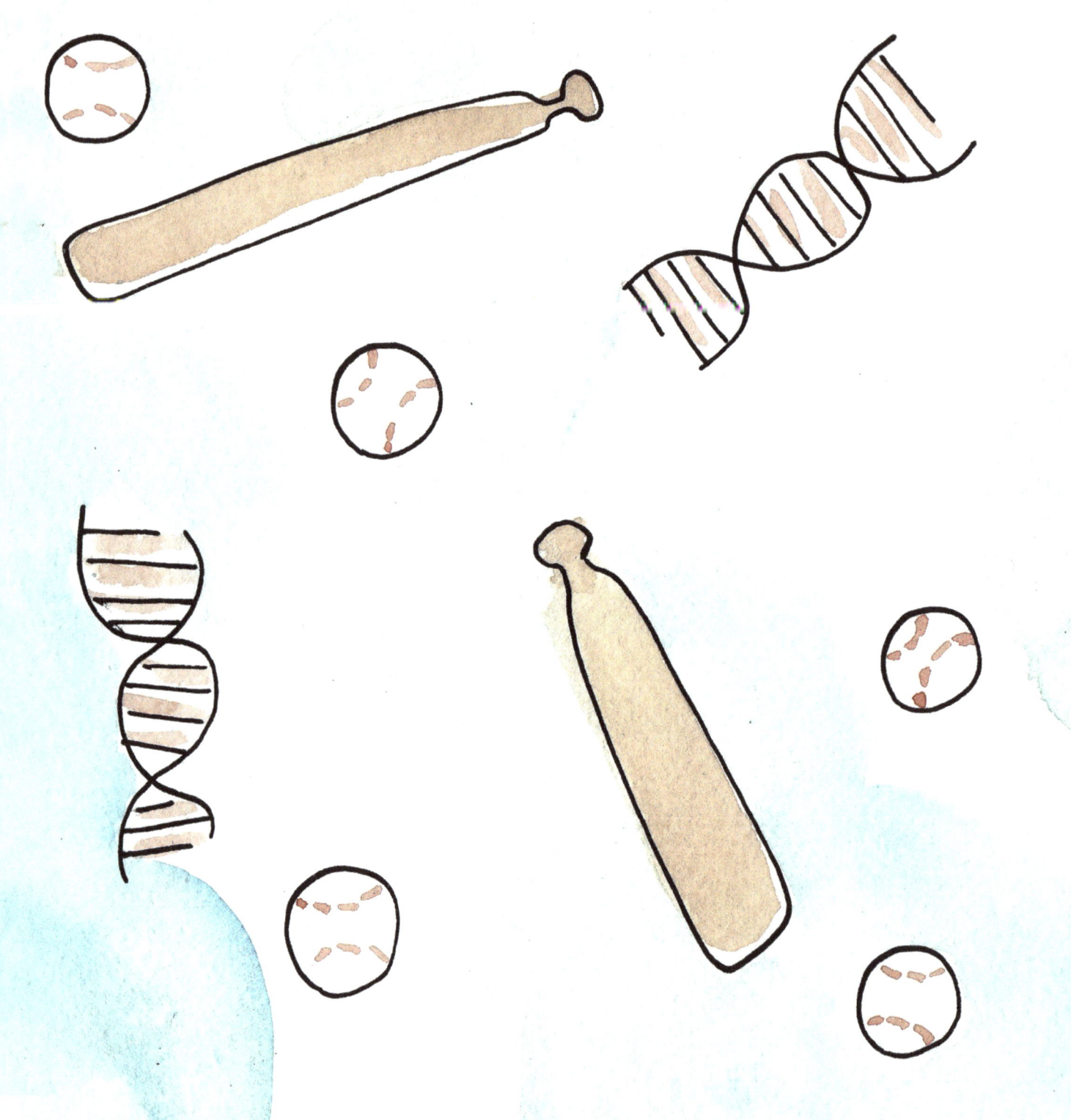

CPSIA information can be obtained
at www.ICGtesting.com
Printed in the USA
LVHW072257110721
692447LV00002B/11